this book is presented to

_____

by

_____

date

_____

_____

_____

_____

One word comes to mind when I think of Easter – Joy.
Joy that is brought into our hearts and lives through the resurrection and the promise and
hope it gives each of us. Aside from the risen Savior, one person has brought more Joy into my life
than any other. This book is dedicated to that person. Others know her as Joyce
but to me she has always been – Joy.

Copyright 2009 by Cane Creek Publishers, LLC

Printed in Reynosa, Tamaulipas Mexico
February 2012
3 4 5 6 7 8 9/16 15 14 13 12

the True Night before Easter

Timothy Penland

illustrated by Savannah Joy Adams

He is Risen!

Timothy Penland

'Twas the night before Easter
Peter lay in his bed,
He just couldn't sleep
For the thoughts in his head.

So much had happened
In the last several days.
Now it all ran together,
It seemed like a maze.

He met this man – Jesus
Through Andrew his brother
Jesus traveled the country
Along with His mother.

Some called Him the Christ
Some thought He was lazy,
Some said He was wise
Others said, "That man's crazy."

Wherever He went
Folks crowded the street,
When He stopped anywhere
Children flocked to his feet.

Most everyone liked Him
And thought He was good,
But a few got so mad
They'd kill if they could.

He healed many sick
Raised some that were dead,
Said, "Don't hate each other –
Love others instead!"

Then a few days ago
As He rode into town,
Many came out to greet Him,
Some even bowed down.

People laid down palm branches
Children sang joyful songs,
But the leaders were angry
They were scared of the throngs.

They said, "This man's evil"
They thought He should die,
They had a fake trial
And paid some men to lie.

Then they sent Him to Pilate
Saying, "Kill Him for us"
"It's you we will follow,
It's you that we trust".

"Don't hurt this good man,"
Pilate heard from his wife.
So he tried to find some way
To save Jesus' life.

But the Chief Priest and scribes
Had started a riot.
The people were shouting
And would not be quiet.

They screamed, "Just kill Jesus
That's what you should do
You can blame it on us,
He's no King of the Jews."

Pilate finally gave in
He sent Jesus to die.
He'd be nailed to a cross
That was raised to the sky.

Jesus died on that day
And was laid in a tomb.
As Peter remembered
His heart filled with gloom.

He also recalled
That Jesus had said,
He would die for our sins
But he would not stay dead.

He said he was dying
To pay for our sin
And, that if He was right
They'd see Him again.

Now three days had passed,
Peter was there when He died.
And he started to wonder
If Jesus had lied.

Then just before dawn
He heard someone outside.
He wanted to see
But he thought he should hide.

When he went to the door
There stood his friend Mary
She was screaming and yelling
The story was scary.

She had been to the tomb
She shared what she found
The stone had been moved,
There was no one around.

Peter stood there bewildered
By what Mary said,
Then John yelled, "Let's see!"
And he took off ahead.

When they got to the tomb
Both men went inside,
Jesus' body was gone
That could not be denied.

Mary also came back
To the garden grave
She was crying and sad
As she looked in the cave.

Then she noticed a man
A gardener she thought
She went to tell him
It was Jesus she sought.

The man looked at Mary
"Please help me!" she said.
Then He whispered her name
And she lifted her head.

Could it really be Jesus?
Was He standing this close?
She just fell at His feet.
He's alive! He arose!

He has risen! He has risen!
The disciples soon heard
And they told everyone
This glorious word!

Jesus died for our sins
But then he arose
He was really God's Son
Now everyone knows.

His promise is simple
His message is true
The tomb now is empty
He's alive just for you!

Acknowledgments

Since starting down the "author/publisher" highway, there have been many stop signs and more than a few bumps in the road. As is the case with any journey, the trip has been made much easier by the fact that I have had companions along the way.

Some like Joy, Ben, Angie and Brett have ridden with me every mile of the way. Special friends like Kirk Hawkins, Mike Miller, Sharon Faloon, Tyson Hamrick, Bruce Frank, and Carl Setterlind have provided the expertise, direction, and/or advice to make sure we stayed on the straight and narrow.

Still others have provided the encouragement, kind word or note at just the right moment and thereby gave us the fuel we needed to continue. Some many more have loved our Christmas book and motivated us to see this "twin" become a reality.

Once again, Savannah has given her special insight to bring the story to life so it becomes more than just words on a page. What a delight to see how she views this incredible story. As before, Angie's guidance and encouragement to Savannah cannot be overstated.

The Easter story is one of tragedy turned into triumph, loss becoming gain, and death giving way to life. Thank you, Lord for the willingness to experience all that this story relates so that we can experience all that these events provide - to us your children.

Timothy Penland

Scripture References

Luke 24:1-12	John 20:1-31	Matt. 4:18-20
John 1:40-41	Mark 6:53-56	John 2:1-12
Matt. 12:1-12	Matt. 14:13-14	Matt. 19:13-15
Matt. 15:29-31	Luke 6:27-31	John 11:1-44
John 12: 12-19	Mark 14: 53-59	John 18: 28-40
Matt. 27:19-31	Matt. 27:57-61	John 2:18-22